Veggie Lover's Crock Pot: 60 Simple & #Delish Slow Cooker Recipes for Veggies

RHONDA BELLE

Copyright © 2016 Rhonda Belle
All rights reserved.

ISBN-13: 978-1539917991

ISBN-10: 1539917991

DEDICATION

To Foodies Everywhere...Enjoy & Be Well!

Table of Contents

A Veggie Lover's Delight... 8
- Apple Brown Betty 8
- Apple Cranberry Crumble 9
- Apple-Sauced Sauerkraut 9
- Artichoke & Cheese Dip 9
- Asparagus Casserole 9
- Aztec Black Beans 10
- Barley with Mushrooms & Green Onions 10
- Black Bean Chili 10
- Broccoli & Cheese Soup 11
- Broccoli Crock-Pot Casserole 11
- Broccoli Pasta 11
- Cheddar Potato Slices 11
- Cheesy Creamed Corn 12
- Chili Con-Queso 12
- Chocolate Peanut Butter Cake 12
- Cream of Sweet Potato Soup 12
- Creamy Spinach Noodle Casserole 13
- Crock-Pot Baked Beans 13
- Crock-Pot Creamed Red Potatoes 14
- Easy Chocolate Clusters 14
- Easy Fruit Dessert 14
- Eggplant Parmigiana 14
- Ginger Brown Bread 15
- Green Bean & Potato Casserole 15
- Green Pepper Boats 16
- Heath Healthy Casserole 16
- Hot Artichoke Dip 16
- Indian Summer Pudding 17
- Italian Green Beans 17
- Italian-Style Veggie Simmer 17
- Macaroni Pie 18
- Meatless Spaghetti Sauce 18
- Mixed Vegetable Bake 18
- Orange Glazed Carrots 19

Perky Paprika Bake	19
Pudding Cake	19
Pumpkin Bread	20
Red Cabbage	20
Refried Bean Dip	20
Rhubarb Bake	21
Rice Pudding	21
Savory Salsa-Corn Cake	21
Slow Cooker Corn Chowder	22
Slow Cooker Scrabble	22
Spaghetti Squash	23
Spicy Salsa Dip	23
Spoon Peaches	23
Squash Casserole	24
Sunshine Squash	24
Sweet & Sour Cabbage	25
Sweet Potato & Pineapple Pudding	25
Sweetly Stewed Tomatoes	25
Swiss Cheese Scalloped Potatoes	26
Vegetable Curry	26
Vegetable Pasta	27
Veggie Chili	27
Veritable Vegetable Soup	28
Wild Rice Casserole	28
Zucchini Bread	29
Zucchini Casserole	29

ACKNOWLEDGEMENTS

To the love of my life, Johnny.
You are Mommy's greatest inspiration.

To my Mom & Dad (Sunset February 2016).
Love you always...

A Veggie Lover's Delight...

Opening the front door on a cold winter evening and being greeted by the inviting smells of soup wafting from a slow cooker can be a dream come true. But the slow cooker/crock-pot can be used year round for yummy, fuss-free meals that don't require heat from a hot oven. At any time of year, a slow cooker can make life more convenient by using less energy and saving time.

Slow cookers come in various sizes and cook food slowly at lower temperatures than conventional methods. For veggies, this can help preserve healthy nutrients. The direct heat from the pot, lengthy cooking and steam created within the tightly-covered container work with the high moisture content in produce, resulting in a wide variety of tasty and heart healthy dishes.

Slow cooking is simple. Always begin with a clean cooker, clean utensils and hands and a clean work area. Read the recipe in advance, cut up vegetables and store them separately in the refrigerator. Keep Pam or nonstick cooking spray handy to grease the liner of the pot if necessary. Always keep any perishable foods refrigerated until preparation time.

Take care to fill your cooker no less than half full and no more than two-thirds full. Vegetables cook slowly so you always want them at the very bottom. For all day cooking, use your lowest slow cooker or crock-pot setting.
Food will stay safe to eat as long as the cooker is operating. Refrigerate leftovers and keep pot tightly covered.

Enjoy these wonderfully simple and #delish recipes crafted just for veggie lovers like you!

Apple Brown Betty
1/8 teaspoon salt
¼ teaspoon nutmeg
½ cup butter or margarine, melted
½ teaspoon cinnamon
¾ cup brown sugar
10 slices of bread, cubed (about 4 cups)
3 lbs. baking apples
Wash apples, peel, core, cut into eighths; place in bottom of slow cooker. Combine bread cubes, cinnamon, nutmeg, salt, sugar, butter; toss together. Place on top of apples. Cover. Cook on low setting 2-4 hours. #Delish!

Apple Cranberry Crumble
¼ teaspoon salt
¾ cup brown sugar
1 cup cranberries
1 teaspoon cinnamon
1/3 cup butter, softened
1/3 cup quick cooking oats
3 crisp Gala apples
Peel, core and slice apples. Place apple slices and cranberries in slow cooker. Mix all remaining ingredients in a separate bowl and sprinkle over top of apple and cranberries. Place 4 or 5 paper towels over the top of the slow cooker, place a wooden spoon across the top of the slow cooker to allow glass lid to vent. Cook on high for 2 hours. #Enjoy!

Apple-Sauced Sauerkraut
½ teaspoon caraway seeds
1 tablespoon butter or margarine
2 cups sweetened applesauce
4 cups sauerkraut, rinsed and drained
Combine all ingredients. Grease sides of slow cooker and place ingredients inside. Set slow cooker to low and let simmer for 1- 1.5 hours. Enjoy!

Artichoke & Cheese Dip
1 cup (8½ oz.) artichoke hearts, drained and chopped
1 cup (8 ounce jar) mayonnaise
1 cup grated parmesan
1 lb. shredded mozzarella
Minced onions
Mix ingredients together. Bake in a lightly buttered slow cooker for about 1 hour. Serve with French bread pieces or wheat crackers. #Delish!

Asparagus Casserole
½ cup coarsely crushed saltines or Ritz crackers
1 can (10 ounces) cream of celery soup
1 cup grated cheddar cheese
1 teaspoon butter
2 cans (10 ounces) sliced asparagus
2 hard cooked eggs, thinly sliced
Place drained asparagus in lightly buttered slow cooker. Combine soup and cheese. Top asparagus with sliced eggs, soup mixture, and cracker crumbs. Dot with butter. Cover and cook on low for 4-6 hours. Enjoy!

Aztec Black Beans

1 lb. dried black beans
1 (11 ounce) can Mexican-style corn, drained
2 (10 ounce) cans diced tomatoes with green chili peppers, drained
2 bunches green onions, chopped
2 tomatoes, diced
Cilantro leaves

Rinse black beans, removing any stones or foreign objects. Cover with water, soak all night. In a large bowl, mix together black beans, corn, diced tomatoes with green chili peppers, chopped green onions, and desired amount of cilantro leaves. Add enough water to just cover beans. Cover and cook on low 8-10 hours. #Delish!

Barley with Mushrooms & Green Onions

1 can (14 ½ ounce) roasted garlic chicken broth (about 2 cups)
1 cup barley
2 teaspoons butter or margarine
3 green onions, thinly sliced (about ½ cup)
4 to 6 ounces fresh or canned mushrooms, sliced
Salt or seasoned salt and pepper to taste

Combine all ingredients in slow cooker. Cover and cook on low for 4 to 4½ hours. Enjoy!

Black Bean Chili

¼ tablespoon crushed red pepper flakes
1 (28 ounce) can chopped tomatoes in juice
1 bay leaf
1 lb. dry black beans
1 tablespoon chili powder
1 tablespoon dried oregano
1 tablespoon ground cumin
1 tablespoon red wine vinegar
1 tablespoon soy sauce
2 cans contrasting beans (pinto, garbanzo, great northern, etc.), drained and rinsed
2 cup water
2 onions, chopped
2 tablespoon oil
6 garlic cloves, minced or pressed
6 ounce can tomato paste

Rinse and sort the beans (do not presoak) and place in the slow cooker with a generous amount of water. Cook on low overnight. In the morning drain the cooking water. Heat the oil in a skillet and sauté the onions, garlic and red pepper flakes. Cook 1 minute, then add chili powder and cumin and cook 2 minutes, stirring. Add this mixture to the slow cooker along with all remaining ingredients except canned beans and garnishes. Stir well and cook on low all day. Stir in canned beans an hour or so before serving. Garnish with sour cream or shredded cheese. #Delish!

Broccoli & Cheese Soup
1 (10 ounce) pkg. frozen chopped broccoli, thawed
1 tablespoon flour
2 cup cooked noodles
2 cups shredded American cheese
2 tablespoon butter
3 tablespoon chopped onions
5 ½ cup milk
Salt to taste
Combine all ingredients in slow cooker. Stir well. Cook on low for 4 hours. Enjoy!

Broccoli Crock-Pot Casserole
1 cup cooked rice or noodles
1 package frozen broccoli (or 1 cup fresh), cooked
1 can cream of mushroom soup
1 jar regular or Mexican Cheez Whiz
Put all ingredients in crock-pot and cook on slow for 1 hour or until ready to eat. Enjoy!

Broccoli Pasta
1 medium onion
1 can cream of mushroom soup
1 lb. Velveeta cheese
1 package frozen broccoli & cauliflower
1 package of shell noodles
Mix onion, cream of mushroom soup and Velveeta in a slow cooker on high until melted. Add broccoli and cauliflower until hot. Add cooked shells right before serving. #Delish!

Cheddar Potato Slices
½ teaspoon paprika
½ teaspoon pepper
1 can (10¾ ounces) cream of mushroom soup
1 cup shredded cheddar cheese
4 medium baking potatoes (about 1¼ pounds), sliced ¼ inch thick
Mix soup, paprika and pepper. Arrange potatoes in greased slow cooker in overlapping rows. Sprinkle with cheese. Spoon soup mixture over cheese. Cover

and cook on high for 3-4 hours, until potatoes are tender. Keep warm (on low) for serving. Enjoy!

Cheesy Creamed Corn
1 (3 ounce) package cream cheese
1 (8 ounce) package cream cheese
2 tablespoons sugar
3 (16 ounce) packages frozen corn
3 tablespoons milk
3 tablespoons water
4 tablespoons butter
6 slices American cheese

Combine all ingredients in slow cooker, mix well. Cover and cook for 4-5 hours on low or until heated through and cheese is melted. Stir well before serving. Enjoy!

Chili Con-Queso
¾ cup cheddar cheese, grated
1 (15½ ounce) tomatoes, chopped, undrained
1 can jalapeno peppers, chopped
1 jar pimiento, chopped, drained
1 medium onion, chopped
2 tablespoons butter
Salt and pepper, to taste

Sauté onion in butter in medium saucepan. Combine next 3 ingredients with onion. Heat to boiling, let simmer for 10-15 minutes to meld the flavors. Add cheese, mixing thoroughly until melted. Serve immediately. Enjoy!

Chocolate Peanut Butter Cake
1/3 cup creamy peanut butter
½ cup chopped nuts
½ cup water
2 cup chocolate cake mix

Combine all ingredients in bowl mixing well. Beat about 2 minutes. Pour batter into a greased and floured 2 pound coffee can. Place can in crock-pot/slow cooker. Cover top of can with 8 paper towels. Cover slow cooker and bake on high for 2-3 hours. Simple and #dclish!

Cream of Sweet Potato Soup
1/8 teaspoon each of ground cloves and nutmeg
1 teaspoon sugar
1½ cup light cream, half-and-half, or milk
2 cups chicken bouillon
3 sweet potatoes, peeled and sliced

Salt to taste

Place sweet potatoes and bouillon in slow cooker. Cover and cook on high for 2-3 hours or until potatoes are tender. Puree potatoes in a blender and return to slow cook along with the remaining ingredients. Cover and cook on high for 1 to 2 hours. Serve hot or chilled with a dollop of sour cream if desired. #Delish!

Creamy Spinach Noodle Casserole

1/3 cup all-purpose flour
1 dash hot pepper sauce
1½ cups cottage cheese
1½ cups sour cream
2 tablespoons vegetable oil
2 teaspoon garlic salt
2 teaspoon Worcestershire sauce
4 green onions, minced
8 ounces dry spinach noodles

Cook noodles in a pot of salted, boiling water until just tender. Drain and rinse with cold water. Toss with vegetable oil. Combine sour cream and flour in a large bowl, mixing well. Stir in cottage cheese, green onions, Worcestershire sauce, hot pepper sauce and garlic salt. Fold noodles into mixture until well combined. Generously grease the inside of a slow cooker and pour in noodle mixture. Cover and cook on high for 1 ½ to 2 hours. Enjoy!

Crock-Pot Baked Beans

½ cup brown sugar
¾ cup maple syrup
1 can chick peas
1 cup molasses
2 cans black beans
2 cans cannellini beans
2 cans red kidney beans
2 diced onions
2 tablespoons prepared mustard

Rinse and drain beans and set aside. On the bottom of the crock-pot place diced onions, then dump on beans. *Do not mix beans.* Next, drizzle on all other ingredients. Slow cook on high for 5-6 hours, stirring once about ¾ of the way through. #Delish!

Crock-Pot Creamed Red Potatoes

1 can cream of potato soup, undiluted
1 envelope ranch salad dressing mix
2 (8 ounces) package of cream cheese, softened
2 lbs. small red potatoes, quartered

Place potatoes in slow cooker. In a small bowl, beat cream cheese, soup and salad dressing; mix well. Stir into potatoes. Cover and cook on low for 8 hours or until potatoes are tender. Also add about a tablespoon of milk and stir before serving. Turn off slow cooker Let sit for 10 minutes or so. #Delish!

Easy Chocolate Clusters

1 jar (24 ounces) dry roasted peanuts
1 package (4 ounces) German sweet chocolate
2 cups semisweet chocolate chips
2 pounds white candy coating, broken into small pieces

In a slow cooker, combine candy coating, German chocolate and chocolate chips. Cover and cook on high for 1 hour; reduce heat to low. Cover and cook 1 hour longer or until melted, stirring every 15 minutes. Add peanuts and mix well. Drop by the teaspoonful onto waxed paper; let stand until set. Store at room temperature. #Delish!

Easy Fruit Dessert

1 can (11 ounces) mandarin orange, sections, drained
1 can (16 ounces) fruit cocktail, well drained
1 can (16 ounces) sliced peaches, well drained
1 can (20 ounces) pineapple chunks, well drained
1 can (21 ounces) cherry pie filling
1 tablespoon lemon juice
3 bananas, sliced
3 grapefruit, peeled and sectioned

Place all ingredients in slow cooker. Toss gently. Cover and cook on low about 4 hours. #Delish!

Eggplant Parmigiana

1/3 cup seasoned bread crumbs
1/3 cup water
½ cup parmesan cheese
1 can marinara sauce
1 pound mozzarella cheese, sliced
2 eggs
3 tablespoons flour
4 large eggplants
Extra-virgin olive oil

Pare each eggplant and cut in ½ inch slices; place in bowl in layers and sprinkle each layer with salt and let stand 30 minutes to drain excess water; dry on paper towels. Mix egg with water and flour. Dip eggplant slices in mixture, drain slightly. Sauté a few slices at a time quickly in hot olive oil. Combine seasoned bread crumbs with the Parmesan cheese. In removable liner, layer one-fourth of the eggplant, top with one-fourth of the crumbs, one-fourth of the marinara sauce and ¼ of the mozzarella cheese. Repeat three times to make four layers of eggplant, crumbs, sauce and mozzarella cheese. Place liner in base. Cover and cook on low 4-5 hours. Enjoy!

Ginger Brown Bread
¼ cup yellow corn meal
½ cup raisins
1 (14 ounce) package gingerbread mix
1 teaspoon salt
1½ cups milk

Combine gingerbread mix with corn meal and salt in large bowl; stir in milk until mixture is evenly moist. Beat at medium speed with electric mixer for 2 minutes. Stir in raisins. Pour into a greased and floured 7 cup mold. Cover with foil and tie. Put a trivet or metal rack in slow cooker. Pour 2 cups hot water into the pot. Place the filled mold on the rack or the trivet (make a ring of alumni foil to rest the mold on if you don't have a slow cooker rack). Cover the pot and cook on high for 3-4 hours or until the bread is done. Remove from pot and cool on a rack for 5 minutes. Loosen the edges with a knife and turn out on a rack and cool slightly. Serve warm with butter or cream cheese. #Delish!

Green Bean & Potato Casserole
½ teaspoon black pepper
1 can cream of chicken soup, undiluted
1 large onion, sliced
1 teaspoon dried dill weed
1 teaspoon salt
4 to 6 medium red-skinned potatoes, sliced about ¼ inch
6 cups fresh trimmed and cut green beans (about 2 pounds)
Cheese sauce of choice (Velveeta or otherwise)
Margarine

Spray the cooker liner with cooking spray or lightly grease with butter or margarine. Layer sliced potatoes, sliced onion and green beans, sprinkling with dill and salt and pepper as you go. Dot with margarine, about 1 tablespoon total, and add about 2 tablespoons of water. Place liner in slow cooker and cover and cook on high for 4 hours (or low for 8 hours). Stir in soup or sauce; turn to lowest setting and cook an additional 30 minutes. #Delish!

Green Pepper Boats

¼ cup chopped onions
¼ cup salsa
¼ teaspoon salt
½ teaspoon pepper
1 can (14.5 ounces) diced tomatoes
1 can (15 ounces) red kidney beans, drained and rinsed
1 package (10 ounces) frozen corn kernels
1 teaspoon Worcestershire sauce
1½ cups cooked rice
2 cups shredded reduced fat cheddar cheese, divided
6 green peppers, tops removed and fully seeded

Combine all ingredients, except ¼ cup cheese and green peppers. Stuff peppers. Arrange peppers in a slow cooker. Cover, cook on low for 6-8 hours or on high for 3-4 hours. Sprinkle with ¼ cup cheese during the last 30 minutes. Serve hot. #Delish!

Heath Healthy Casserole

¼ cup green pepper, diced
1 onion, diced
1 pint tomato juice
1 tablespoon sugar
1 teaspoon salt
2 cups carrots, cut in strips, cooked & drained
2 cups celery, diced
3 tablespoons tapioca
4 cups green beans, drained
Dash of pepper

Mix all ingredients together in slow cooker. Dot with 2 tablespoons margarine and cook on low for 8-10 hour or on high for 4-5 hours. #Delish!

Hot Artichoke Dip

1/8 teaspoon garlic powder
1/3 cup mayonnaise
1/3 cup sour cream
½ cup parmesan cheese, grated
1 tablespoon pimento, diced
6 ounces artichoke hearts, marinated

Drain and chop artichoke hearts. Combine all ingredients and place in a slow cooker. Cover and heat 30 to 60 minutes until hot and well mixed. Serve with tortilla chips or assorted crackers. #Delish!

Indian Summer Pudding

¼ cup light brown sugar
¼ teaspoon allspice
1/3 cup molasses
½ cup cornmeal
½ teaspoon cinnamon
½ teaspoon ginger
½ teaspoon salt
2 tablespoon butter
3 cup milk
3 large eggs

Lightly grease walls of slow cooker. Preheat on high for 20 minutes. Meanwhile bring milk, cornmeal and salt to a boil. Boil, stirring constantly, for 5 minutes. Cover and simmer for an additional 10 minutes. In a large bowl, combine remaining ingredients. Gradually beat in hot cornmeal mixture and whisk until smooth. Pour into slow cooker and cook on high for 2-3 hours or low for 6-8 hours. Enjoy!

Italian Green Beans

½ cup Parmesan cheese
½ teaspoon basil &/or oregano
1/4½ teaspoon onion &/or garlic powders
1 (15 ounces) can stewed tomatoes, chopped
3 (1 lb.) cans Italian style green beans (2 of them drained)
4 cans (8 ounces) sliced mushrooms, undrained

Add all ingredients except green beans. Mix thoroughly and simmer for 15 minutes. Add green beans and mix. Slow cook on lowest setting for up to 3 hours. #Delish!

Italian-Style Veggie Simmer

1½ cups mozzarella cheese, shredded
1 large onion, sliced thinly
1 medium eggplant, cut in 1" cubes
1 tablespoon olive oil
1 teaspoon oregano
1 teaspoon salt
12 ounces fresh mushrooms, sliced
2 cups tomato sauce
2 to 3 medium zucchini, halved & sliced ½"
4 plum tomatoes, sliced ¼" thick
Salt and pepper, to taste

Toss eggplant and zucchini with the 1 teaspoon of salt. Place in a large colander over a bowl to drain for about 1 hour. Drain and squeeze excess moisture out. In a large skillet over medium heat, sauté onion, eggplant, zucchini, and mushrooms until slightly tender. In the slow cooker, layer 1/3 of the veggies (including sliced tomatoes), 1/3 of the tomato sauce and 1/3 of the cheese. Sprinkle with oregano, salt and pepper. Repeat layering at least two more times. Cover and cook on low 6-8 hours. Serve over rice or pasta and enjoy!

Macaroni Pie
¼ cup margarine
1 (16 ounces) can of evaporated milk
1 (8 ounce) box elbow macaroni, cooked
1 teaspoon sugar
1½ cup sweet milk
2 eggs
3 cups grated cheese
Salt and pepper to taste

Combine cooked macaroni with other ingredients and pour into a greased slow cooker. Cook for 3½ hours on lowest setting.

Meatless Spaghetti Sauce
½ teaspoon oregano
½ teaspoon pepper
½ teaspoon red pepper, optional
½ cup sugar
1 (15½ ounces) can tomato sauce
1 (29 ounces) can tomato puree
1 (6 ounces) can tomato paste
1 small onion, finely chopped
1 teaspoon salt
1½ cups water

Sauté onion until tender. Add onion, puree, sauce, paste, water, salt, pepper and oregano to slow cooker and set to lowest setting. Cook for 10 hours. Enjoy!

Mixed Vegetable Bake
½ cup mayonnaise
½ teaspoon salt
1 (17 ounces) can tomatoes
1 teaspoon basil
1 teaspoon tarragon
2 cans (17 ounces each) creamed corn
2 cans (16 ounces each) green beans, cut
2 cans (16 ounces) peas
Pepper to taste

Combine all ingredients in removable slow cooker liner, mix well to blend herbs. Place liner in base, cover with lid and cook on low for 4-6 hours. #Delish!

Orange Glazed Carrots

¼ teaspoon salt
2 cups water
2 tablespoons chopped pecans
3 cups thinly sliced carrots
3 tablespoons butter or margarine
3 tablespoons orange marmalade

Combine carrots, water, and salt in slow cooker. Cover and cook on high for 2-3 hours or until the carrots are done. Drain well; stir in remaining ingredients. Cover and cook on high 20-30 minutes. #Delish!

Perky Paprika Bake

2 large onions, sliced thin
3 tablespoons paprika
5 large carrots, cubed
5 large celery stalks
8 large potatoes, cubed
Salt & pepper to taste

Throw all ingredients into the slow cooker, add water to the top of the veggies and cook on high for 4 hours. #Delish!

Pudding Cake

¼ cup oil
¼ cup unsweetened cocoa
½ cup chocolate syrup
½ cup coarsely chopped pecans, or walnuts
½ cup milk
½ cup sugar
½ teaspoon salt
1 cup boiling water
1 cup flour
1 teaspoon vanilla extract
2 teaspoons baking powder
Whipped cream or ice cream

Mix together flour, sugar, nuts, cocoa, baking powder, and salt. Stir in milk, oil and vanilla. Mix boiling water and chocolate syrup. Pour over batter. Place a mall trivet in the bottom of slow cooker; add 2 cups warm water. Pour mixture into a 6 cup mold and place mold in a cooker and cover with 4 layers of paper towels. Cover cooker and cook on high for 3-4 hours. Serve warm with cream. #Delish!

Pumpkin Bread

½ cup brown sugar, firmly packed
½ cup canned pumpkin
1 cup all-purpose flour
1 teaspoon pumpkin pie spice
1½ teaspoon baking powder
2 eggs
2 tablespoons vegetable oil
4 tablespoons raisins or dried currants, finely chopped

In small bowl combine flour, baking powder and pumpkin pie spice; set aside. In a medium mixing bowl combine brown sugar and oil; beat till well combined. Beat in eggs. Add pumpkin; mix well. Add flour mixture. Beat just until combined. Stir in raisins. Pour pumpkin mixture into 2 well-greased and floured ½ pint straight-sided canning jars. Cover jars tightly with greased foil. Place a piece of crumpled foil in slow cooker liner. Place jars atop crumpled foil. Cover; cook on high setting for 1-½ to 1-¾ hours or until a wooden toothpick inserted near centers comes out clean. Remove jars from the cooker; cool 10 minutes in jars. Remove bread from jars. Cool thoroughly on wire rack. Makes 2 loaves. Enjoy!

Red Cabbage

2/3 cup cider vinegar
1 large head of red cabbage, washed and coarsely sliced
2 cups hot water
2 medium onions coarsely chopped
2 teaspoon salt
3 tablespoon sugar
6 tablespoon butter
6 tart apples, cored & quartered

Place all ingredients in slow cooker in the order listed. Cover and cook on low for 8-10 hours (high for 3 hours). Stir well before serving. #Delish!

Refried Bean Dip

¼ teaspoon salt
½ cup chopped green onions
1 (20 ounces) can refried beans
1 (4 ounces) can chopped green chilies
1 cup shredded cheddar cheese
2 tablespoons bottled taco sauce
Tortilla chips

In a slow cooker, combine beans with cheese, chilies, onions, salt, and taco sauce. Cover and cook on low for 2 to 2-½ hours. Serve hot from the pot. #Delish!

Rhubarb Bake
¼ cup butter or margarine
1/3 cup flour
1/3 cup sugar
¾ cup sugar
1¾ cup fresh rhubarb
1 cinnamon stick, grated
1 teaspoon grated lemon peel
2 whole cloves

Cut rhubarb into small pieces. Combine rhubarb with ¾ cup sugar, cinnamon, cloves and lemon peel in cooker. Cover and cook on low for 3-4 hours. Remove whole spices. Spoon rhubarb into baking dish. Combine remaining ingredients and sprinkle over rhubarb. Bake on high for 20 to 25 minutes. #Delish!

Rice Pudding
½ cup dried apricots or peaches, minced
½ cup raisins
2/3 cup white or brown sugar
1 teaspoon cinnamon
1 teaspoon nutmeg
1 teaspoon salt
1½ cup scalded milk
2 tablespoon vanilla
2½ cup cooked rice
3 eggs, beaten
3 tablespoon soft butter

Combine all ingredients and poured into lightly greased slow cooker liner. Cook on high 1-2 hours; stir during first 30 minutes. #Delish!

Savory Salsa-Corn Cake
½ cup sour cream
1 can (15 ounces) creamed corn
1 can (4 ounces) chopped green chilies, undrained
2 boxes (8 ounces each) corn muffin mix
2 eggs
2 tablespoons soft margarine
3 to 4 tablespoons chunky salsa

In a medium bowl, combine creamed corn, eggs, sour cream, chilies, and margarine. Whisk together until well combined. Add corn muffin mix, stirring well to combine. Generously grease a slow cooker with margarine or butter. Pour batter into the cooker. Spoon salsa over the top and cut into the batter. Cover and cook on high for about 2½ hours. Turn heat off and let cool with lid ajar, for about 15 minutes. Loosen sides with a knife and invert onto a large plate. If a little of the top sticks to the bottom of the pot, dollop a little salsa on the top, or decorate with sour cream and chopped green onion. #Delish!

Slow Cooker Corn Chowder

½ stick butter
1 large onion, diced
1 teaspoon salt
2 large potatoes, cut into 1" chunks
2 pints half and half
3 (16 ounces) cans of corn, drained
Pepper to taste

Put everything except the dairy products in the cooker and cook on low for 7-8 hours. Move to a blender, and puree. Return to cooker add the half & half and butter; stir. Cook on high for one hour. Stir and serve. #Delish!

Slow Cooker Scrabble

1/3 cup melted butter
1/3 cup Worcestershire sauce
½ teaspoon seasoned salt
1 13 ounce can or jar of salted peanuts or asst. mixed nuts
1 teaspoon celery salt
1 teaspoon garlic salt
2 cups corn Chex
2 cups rice Chex
2 cups wheat Chex
2 tablespoons grated parmesan cheese
3 cups thin pretzel sticks

In large (double) paper bag, mix together pretzels, cereals, and nuts along with the garlic salt, celery salt, seasoned salt, and grated cheese. Empty bag into large mixing bowl and sprinkle the melted butter and Worcestershire sauce over all mixing gently with your hands. Empty bowl into slow cooker and cook on low for 3-4 hours. Tear open paper bags you used to originally mix the scrabble and spread them out onto a counter. Spread heated scrabble mixture onto torn open bags and let dry for a minimum of one hour letting the paper absorb any excess moisture. Store in airtight containers for up to 2 or 3 weeks. #Delish!

Spaghetti Squash

1 spaghetti squash
2 cups water
Parmesan cheese
Salt and pepper to taste

With a skewer or large fork, puncture several holes in the squash. Pour water in the slow cooker, add the whole squash. Cover and cook on low for 8-9 hours. Split and remove seeds, then transfer the "spaghetti" strands to a bowl. Serve tossed with butter and salt and pepper, Parmesan cheese or your favorite sauce. Enjoy!

Spicy Salsa Dip

1 package picante sauce or salsa
1 pound Velveeta cheese spread, cubed
1 can Rotel chilies and tomatoes
2 tablespoons cilantro

Place brick of Velveeta, salsa or picante and Rotel into slow cooker and turn on highest setting, stirring occasionally until melted and blended. Stir in all other ingredients when melted. Serve with tortilla chips and enjoy!

Spoon Peaches

1/3 cup sugar
½ can evaporated milk
½ cup brown sugar
¾ cup Bisquik
¾ teaspoon cinnamon
2 cups peaches, mashed
2 eggs
2 teaspoons margarine, melted
2 teaspoons vanilla

Spray slow cooker with non-stick cooking spray. Combine sugars and Bisquik. Add eggs and vanilla. Mix. Add margarine and milk. Mix. Add peaches and cinnamon. Pour into slow cooker and cook on low for 6-8 hours. #Delish!

Squash Casserole

½ cup butter or margarine, melted
1 can cream of chicken soup
1 cup sour cream
2 slices bread, cubed
5 cups yellow squash, canned or frozen

Place squash in slow cooker with butter and cook on high for 1 hour. Add undiluted soup and cook until hot. Add bread and sour cream and cook until bubbly. #Delish!

¼ cup finely chopped nuts
¼ cup packed brown sugar
1 box pound cake mix
1 tablespoon flour
1 teaspoon cinnamon

Mix cake mix according to package directions. Pour batter into a well-greased and floured 2 pound coffee tin. Combine sugar, flour, nuts and cinnamon and sprinkle over cake batter. Place can in slow cooker atop a trivet or ring of aluminum foil. Cover top of can with 8 layers of paper towels. Cover pot and bake on high 3-4 hours. Slide hot cake out of can and onto a plate to cut and serve. #Delish!

Sunshine Squash

¼ teaspoon black pepper
½ cup chicken broth
½ teaspoon salt
1 butternut squash, about 2 pounds, peeled, seeded and diced
1 can (14½ ounces) tomatoes, undrained
1 can (about 15 ounces) corn, drained
1 can green chilies, coarsely chopped
1 clove garlic, minced well
1 green bell pepper, seeded and cut into 1" pieces
1 medium onion, coarsely chopped
1 tablespoon plus 1½ teaspoons tomato paste

Combine all ingredients except tomato paste in slow cooker. Cover and cook on low for 6 hours or until squash is tender. Remove about ¼ cup cooking liquid and blend with tomato paste. Stir into slow cooker. Cook for 30 minutes or until mixture is slightly thickened and heated through. Serve hot. #Delish!

Sweet & Sour Cabbage

1/8 teaspoon pepper
¼ cup bacon bits
¼ cup packed brown sugar
¼ cup vinegar
¼ cup water
½ teaspoon salt
1 medium head red cabbage, shredded (about 8 cups)
1 small onion, finely chopped
2 tablespoons all-purpose flour

Mix all ingredients in a slow cooker. Cover and cook on low for 6 ½ to 7 hours or until cabbage is tender. Spoon into serving bowl; sprinkle with shredded cheddar if desired. #Delish!

Sweet Potato & Pineapple Pudding

½ tablespoon nutmeg
1 ¼ cups brown sugar, firmly packed
1 can (12 ounces) evaporated milk
1 tablespoon ground cinnamon
2 cans (8 ounces) crushed pineapple in unsweetened juice, undrained
3 eggs, slightly beaten
3 pounds sweet potatoes, peeled and shredded
6 tablespoon margarine or butter, cut in cubes

Lightly grease slow cooker. Combine sweet potatoes, pineapple, evaporated milk, brown sugar, margarine, eggs, cinnamon, and nutmeg. Cover and cook on low 7-8 hours or on high for 4 hours, stirring every 2 hours until the potatoes are tender. Serve hot or at room temperature. #Delish!

Sweetly Stewed Tomatoes

1/8 teaspoon pepper
½ cup green pepper, chopped
¾ cup celery, chopped
1 medium onion, thinly sliced
1 small bay leaf
2 teaspoon salt
2 tablespoons margarine
3 tablespoons sugar
6 to 8 ripe tomatoes

Core tomatoes; place in boiling water for about 15 to 20 seconds, then into ice water to cool quickly; peel. Cut tomatoes in wedges. In slow cooker, combine all ingredients. Cover and cook on low for 8-9 hours. Remove bay leaf. Sprinkle top with parsley, if desired. Serve as a side dish or freeze in portions for soups or other recipes. #Delish!

Swiss Cheese Scalloped Potatoes

¼ cup finely chopped green onion
¼ teaspoon ground nutmeg
¼ teaspoon salt
½ cup yellow onion, finely chopped
½ cup whole milk
2 pounds baking potatoes, peeled and thinly sliced
2 tablespoons all-purpose flour
3 ounces Swiss cheese slices, torn into small pieces
3 tablespoons butter, cubed small

Layer half the potatoes, ¼ cup onion, 1/8 tsp salt, 1/8 tsp nutmeg, and 1 tablespoon butter in slow cooker. Repeat layers. Cover and cook on low for 7 hours or on high for 4 hours. Remove potatoes with slotted spoon to serving dish. Blend milk and flour in small bowl until smooth. Stir mixture into slow cooker. Add cheese; stir to combine. If slow cooker is on low, turn to high, cover and cook until slightly thickened, about 10 minutes. Stir. Pour cheese mixture over potatoes and serve. Garnish with chopped green onions, if desired. #Delish!

Vegetable Curry

1/8 teaspoon ground cinnamon
¼ teaspoon salt
½ teaspoon crushed red pepper
1 cup onion, coarsely chopped
1 teaspoon ground coriander
1 (14 ounce) can vegetable broth
1 (15 ounce) can garbanzo beans, drained
1 (16 ounce) can tomatoes, cut up
2 cups hot cooked rice
2 medium potatoes, cut into ½ cubes
2 tablespoons quick-cooking tapioca
2 teaspoons curry powder
3 to 4 cloves garlic, minced
4 medium carrots, bias sliced into 1 inch slices
8 ounces green beans, cut into 1 pieces

In slow cooker, combine carrots, garbanzo beans, potatoes, green beans, onion, garlic, tapioca, curry powder, coriander, red pepper, salt, and cinnamon. Pour broth over all. Cover; cook on low setting for 8-10 hours or on high-heat setting for 4-5 hours. Stir in undrained tomatoes. Cover; let stand 5 minutes. Serve with cooked rice. Enjoy!

Vegetable Pasta

¼ teaspoon salt
½ teaspoon basil, dried
½ teaspoon pepper
1 cup cream
1 cup mozzarella cheese, shredded
1 cup parmesan cheese, grated
1 package frozen broccoli cuts
1 yellow squash, ¼" sliced
1 zucchini, ¼" sliced
1½ cups fresh mushrooms, sliced
12 ounces fettucine
2 carrots, thinly sliced
2 egg yolks
2 tablespoons butter or margarine
2 to 3 cloves garlic, minced
4 green onions, sliced

Rub slow cooker walls with butter. Put zucchini, yellow squash, carrots, mushrooms, broccoli, onions, garlic, seasonings and parmesan in slow cooker. Cover and cook on high for 2 hours. Cook fettucine according to package directions; drain. Add cooked fettucine, mozzarella, cream and egg yolks. Stir to blend well. Allow to heat for 15 to 30 minutes. For serving, turn to low for up to 30 minutes. #Delish!

Veggie Chili

1 green pepper, seeded and coarsely chopped
1 teaspoon black pepper
1 teaspoon cumin
2 (14 ½ ounces) cans tomatoes, drained
2 (16 ounces) cans red kidney beans, drained
2 cloves garlic, peel and crushed
2 medium onions, coarsely chopped
2-3 tablespoons chili powder
Salt and pepper to taste

Place all ingredients in a slow cooker. Stir well. Cover and cook on low for 10 hours. Enjoy!

Veritable Vegetable Soup

¼ teaspoon salt
¼ teaspoon turmeric
½ cup celery, chopped
½ cup green pepper, chopped
½ teaspoon basil
¾ cup chopped onion
1 large russet potato, diced
1 medium sweet potato, diced
1 teaspoon paprika
1 whole bay leaf
15 ounces chickpeas, rinsed
16 ounces kidney beans
2 tomatoes, chopped
2 garlic cloves, minced
2 teaspoons soy sauce
3 cups chicken broth
Dash of cayenne pepper

In large skillet, sauté onion, celery and pepper until crisp-tender. Add potato and garlic; sauté an additional 3-5 minutes. Transfer slow cooker. Add remaining ingredients. Cover and cook on low for 9-10 hours or until vegetables are tender. Discard bay leaf before serving. #Delish!

Wild Rice Casserole

¼ cup butter or margarine, melted
½ cup wild rice, uncooked
1 bunch green onions, chopped
1 envelope dry onion soup mix
1 tablespoon dried parsley
1½ cup long-grained rice, uncooked
4 cups water
8 ounce fresh or canned mushrooms, sliced

Combine all ingredients. Pour into lightly greased slow cooker. Cover, cook on high 2½ hours, stirring occasionally. Turn off slow cooker and let sit for 10 minutes before serving. #Delish!

Zucchini Bread

¼ teaspoon salt
½ teaspoon baking powder
½ teaspoon nutmeg
½ to 1 cup chopped nuts
2/3 cup vegetable oil
1 teaspoon cinnamon
1¼ cups sugar
1 1/3 cups zucchini, peeled and grated
2 cups flour
2 eggs
2 teaspoons vanilla

With mixer, beat eggs until light and foamy. Add oil, sugar, grated zucchini and vanilla. Mix well. Stir dry ingredients with nuts. Add to zucchini mixture. Mix well. Pour into greased and floured 2 pound coffee can or 2 quart mold. Place into slow cooker liner. Cover top of can or mold with 8 paper towels. Cover and bake on high for 3 to 4 hours. *Do not check or remove cover until last hour of baking.* Let stand 5 minutes and serve. Enjoy!

Zucchini Casserole

¼ cup flour
½ cup butter or margarine, melted
½ medium onion, chopped
1 can (10¼ ounces) cream of chicken soup
1 cup shredded carrot
1 cup sour cream
1 package (8 ounces) seasoned dry breadcrumbs
2 pounds (about 6 cups) zucchini, thinly sliced

In large bowl, combine squash, onion, carrot and soup. Mix sour cream and flour, stir into vegetables. Toss crumbs with butter and place half in slow cooker. Add vegetable mixture and top with remaining stuffing crumbs. Cover and cook on low for 6-8 hours. #Delish!

Thank you for your purchase!
May you enjoy and be well!

ABOUT THE AUTHOR

I am a Tennessee native and a connoisseur of good eats. My culinary delights are inspired by my Southern roots.

I am from cornbread and cabbage, fried chicken and Kool-Aid soaked lemon slices.

I am from hen houses, persimmon trees and juicy, red tomatoes on the vine.

I am from sunflowers growing wild in summer and homemade ice cream in the winter.

I am from family reunions, blue collar men, happy housewives, and Sunday dinners.

I am from spiritual folks who didn't always get it right, but believed in the power of prayer – and taught it to their kids.

I am from the hottest of hot summers and kids running barefoot and free through thirsty Tennessee grass.

I am from a grandmother who sang gospel that was magic...song drenched air would tumble from her lungs, leap into your spirit and make you feel fantastic things.

I am from hard, heartfelt lessons about living and kitchens full of the perfume of love.

♥♥♥ *This book is from my heart to yours.* ♥♥♥

For info, freebies & new book notices, follow @SoDelishDish on social media!
Scan with your smartphone!

FIND MORE BOOKS ONLINE

Printed in Great Britain
by Amazon